Busting Social Media Myths

Separating Fact from Fiction

Table of Contents

The biggest risk is not taking any risk... In a world that is changing really quickly, the only strategy that is guaranteed to fail is not taking risks.

— Mark Zuckerberg

Chapter 1. Introduction

Welcome to our Special Report: "Busting Social Media Myths: Separating Fact from Fiction." This exciting and insightful report is a must-have if you've ever found yourself grappling to decipher the truth in the constantly evolving world of social media. Full of clear, yet comprehensive analysis, this report aims to demystify the common misconceptions clouding our understanding of social media platforms and their function in our lives. Whether you're a novice social media user or a seasoned digital guru, this Report not only confronts the multitude of myths flood the social media landscape but also empowers you with the knowledge to navigate through it confidently. Hooked yet? Turn the pages and dive into a world that dares to ground the chimeric social media galaxy with an enlightening clarity! Be a part of our myth-busting journey, where truth meets technology, and empower yourself in the digital age.

Chapter 2. Understanding Social Media: A Brief Overview

Social media is a sweeping term that encapsulates a variety of digital communication channels. These platforms, built to foster conversation, share information, and establish connections, have steadily transformed the way we relate to the world and each other. Initially adapted as a means of personal expression and relationship building, they've grown to encompass so much more, serving as platforms for news dissemination, business marketing, activism, and creative expression alike.

2.1. Evolution of Social Media

It all began with the concept of 'computer-mediated communication' (CMC). In the 1970s, users could interact with each other through a system of networked computers. However, the birth of what we now understand as social media didn't occur until much later, with platforms like BBS (Bulletin Board System) and 'The WELL' in the 1980s. It was only in the 1990s that we saw the inception of online chatting and the creation of social networking sites like 'Six Degrees'. This was the catalyst that opened the floodgates to the likes of Friendster, Myspace, and finally Facebook, Twitter, Instagram, and Snapchat in the 2000s.

The evolution of social media has also meant a shift from simply being a platform for connecting with friends and family to a utility tool used for diverse purposes. We see this pivot reflected in the advent of LinkedIn, a site designed specifically for professional networking, and YouTube, a platform aimed at democratizing video sharing and viewing. Increasingly, users are turning to social media to stay informed about global events, purchasing decisions, and to participate in democratic processes by expressing their perspectives.

2.2. The Structure and Function of Social Media Platforms

At its core, the architecture of social media is governed by algorithms. Algorithms are formulae or set of rules that social networking sites use to determine what content to show a user and in what order. Often these algorithms are proprietary, and the specifics are kept carefully guarded by social media companies. However, they often prioritize content that appears popular, based on metrics such as 'likes', 'shares', 'comments', or 'retweets'.

Each social media platform functions differently, catering to varying user needs. Facebook, for example, serves as a digital scrapbook of a user's life, hosting photos, status updates and fostering communication between friends and family. Twitter, in contrast, facilitates bite-sized nuggets of information and opinions in a 280-character microblogging format, making it a go-to source for real-time news and trending topics. Instagram, a photo and video sharing social networking service, serves as a repository of visual content catering to personal and professional users. LinkedIn, is aimed at showcasing work experience, displaying professional achievements, and fostering B2B and B2C connections. Each platform's unique function shapes the user behavior and the type of content that predominates.

2.3. The Impact of Social Media

Social media has far-reaching impacts that span across several dimensions. It has significantly changed our communication habits, enabling real-time, global conversations, and amplified individuals' voices to reach a wider audience. It's also a source of entertainment, letting users share and consume a variety of content, from personal anecdotes and life updates to creative videos, music, and artwork.

However, it's worth noting that not all impacts of social media are positive. There are recurring concerns over privacy, personal security, and the spread of misinformation. Moreover, mental health issues related to social media use, such as anxiety, depression, and decreased self-esteem, have been increasingly documented, highlighting a darker underbelly of these platforms.

2.4. Understanding Social Media Etiquette

Just like any social environment, there's an established etiquette on social media. While much of it is intuitive and based on respectful interaction, some elements are unique to the digital realm. Understanding and adhering to this etiquette is crucial for maintaining positive online relationships and ensuring a respectful digital footprint.

In conclusion, understanding social media isn't just about knowing how to post a status update or upload a photo. It's a multi-faceted digital tool that wields immense power. From influencing global discourse and societal norms to impacting personal well-being, it mirrors the complexity of the society it serves. As we continue our journey into the world of social media, it's crucial to develop a nuanced, informed perspective on these platforms, the myths, and realities surrounding their use, and how we can use them for our benefit and the greater good. The subsequent chapters of this book will delve deeper into these issues, separating fact from fiction and offering guidance on conscientious use.

Chapter 3. Decoding Social Media Algorithm Myths

The various social media platforms and their respective algorithms pose a myriad of questions, facades, and often, misconceptions. The objective of this chapter is to illuminate and decode the most common myths surrounding social media algorithms, applying an analytical lens to navigate the discourse of fact and fiction. We will dissect persisting beliefs, debunking them where necessary, and providing comprehensive insights into how these mysterious algorithms actually work.

3.1. The Nature of Algorithms

In the simplest terms, an algorithm is a predefined set of instructions designed to execute specific tasks. Drawn by complex computations, numerous variables, and evolving machine learning protocols, social media algorithms are sophisticated mechanisms that determine what content to show you, when to show it, and how often. Crucially, they feed on engagement - crafting user feeds based on behaviour, preferences, interactions, and more.

However, several misconceptions have come to shadow the concept of these algorithms, prompting misunderstanding and misinterpretation.

3.2. Myth 1: Algorithms Are Biased

One common misconception is that these algorithms harbor biases, showing preferential treatment towards certain users or content. In truth, most algorithms are designed to prioritize content based on user engagement and preference rather than explicit favoritism. A profile or post attracts attention not due to inbuilt bias within the system, but because of the type of engagement it encourages. The algorithms are simply responding to signals received from user interactions. Preference shown by users is often misconstrued as bias on the part of the algorithms.

3.3. Myth 2: Algorithms Suppress Content

The belief that social media algorithms suppress certain types of content or limit their reach is widespread. While controversial content or those against community guidelines may indeed face restrictions, standard posts are not intentionally suppressed. The algorithm primarily works to foster engagement, encouraging posts that are engaging and offering users a personalized feed.

3.4. Myth 3: Everyone Sees the Same Content

Another myth is the idea that all users see the same content on social media platforms. However, the reality is quite different. Algorithms cater to individual user behavior, interactions, preferences, and history. Thus, the content displayed varies drastically from user to user.

3.5. Myth 4: Algorithms Are Static

There is a widely held belief that once an algorithm is set up, it stays the same forever. However, this is a gross oversimplification. In reality, algorithms are constantly changing, evolving and adapting based on a variety of factors such as changing user behavior, emerging trends, platform updates, and technological advancements. Machines learn from new data to amend their reflecting algorithms, resulting in constant tweaks and adjustments.

3.6. Understanding the Algorithm: Factors at Play

Now that we've busted some of the common myths regarding social media algorithms, it would be beneficial to delve into understanding how these mechanisms function.

Their aim is to present each user with a personalized and engaging content, effectively maximizing the time spent on the platform. Key driving factors include:

1. **Relevance**: Based on a user's past activity and engagement, the algorithm determines content relevance to the user. This extends to similar topics, posts from frequently interacted accounts, and content that aligns with expressed interests.

2. **Timeliness**: Recency of content is important. Newly posted content has a high chance of appearing at the top of a user's feed.

3. **Engagement**: Content that garners significant likes, comments, shares, or saves sends strong signals to the algorithm about its popularity and value, influencing its visibility on others' feeds.

4. **Relationships**: If a user frequently interacts with certain accounts, the algorithm assumes a close relationship and is likely to show more of their content.

To understand these algorithms is to appreciate the complexity of social media platforms. It equips us to better utilize these platforms, acknowledging their inner workings. It is, therefore, crucial to separate the myths from the realities, valuing the power and influence of these intelligent systems in a rapidly digitalizing world. With a solid grasp of algorithmic functions, we can ensure our voices are heard in the digital arena, fostering better connection, communication, and understanding in the social media landscape.

Chapter 4. The Real Impact of Social Media on Mental Health

Social media platforms have exploded in popularity, with apps such as Instagram, Facebook, and Twitter becoming an integral part of daily routines. As these virtual spaces continue to evolve, the discussion surrounding their effect on mental health has become increasingly pressing. The following sections aim to demystify some common misconceptions about the impact of social media on mental health and delve into what the research actually tells us.

4.1. Unpacking the Link

Initial impressions of the narratives surrounding social media and its implications often suggest that the platforms are solely destructive to mental health. However, this perspective should be examined critically.

Research has shown a correlation between heavy social media use and mental health issues such as depression, anxiety, and loneliness. Some studies indicate that spending excessive time on social media sites, continually comparing oneself to others and dealing with cyberbullying can indeed be harmful. For instance, a report by the Royal Society for Public Health in the UK ranked Instagram as the worst social media platform for mental health, contributing to anxiety, depression, loneliness, bullying, and poor body image. But it's crucial to remember that correlation does not imply causation. While it's true that those with mental health issues may spend more time on social media, it does not necessarily mean that the platforms themselves are the root cause of these issues.

Moreover, the impact of social media on mental health can vary significantly based on a range of factors such as age, personality, the individual's existing mental health status, and how they use the platform. It isn't a one-size-fits-all model, and understanding these nuances forms a large part of the narrative.

4.2. The Positive Effects

To gain a balanced perspective, it is essential to consider the positive impacts of social media on mental health. Social media serves as a connector, providing a means for individuals to stay in touch with friends and family, join groups with shared interests, and offer support to those in need. For some, it can play a critical role in overcoming feelings of isolation and loneliness, particularly for those who have difficulty in social interactions, like individuals on the autism spectrum or those with social anxiety.

Research has shown that social media can also be used as a tool for positive self-expression and identity formation, particularly among young adults. It provides an outlet for individuals to share their successes, interests, and even struggles, reinforcing their sense of self.

Moreover, platforms like Instagram and Facebook have made concerted efforts to addresses mental health challenges by introducing features like warning labels for potentially harmful content and resources for users exhibiting signs of mental health distress.

4.3. Towards a Balanced Approach

Understanding social media's intricate connection to mental health is a multifaceted challenge. Social media is neither an absolute evil harboring negative consequences for mental health nor is it a panacea for mental health issues. It has the potential to elevate or harm mental well-being, dependent on various factors.

It's about usage management and awareness. This involves setting personal boundaries, analyzing one's behavior patterns, and being aware of potential negative impacts. Understanding when usage turns from constructive to destructive, developing a habit of digital detoxification, and encouraging open conversations about mental health can contribute to a balanced, healthier approach.

Practicing mindful consumption, curating a positive online space, and fostering connections rather than comparisons can help turn the narrative surrounding social media from a harmful obsession to a communal asset.

In conclusion, the impact of social media on mental health is layered and complex. Though it undeniably has its pitfalls, a call for its complete eradication would be a simplistic solution to a nuanced challenge. What's needed is a more sophisticated approach, bolstered by continuous discourse, research, and a concerted effort to nurture a more empathetic, beneficial virtual landscape.

Chapter 5. Dispelling Myths About Privacy and Security on Social Media

The topic of privacy and security on social media is trapped in a web of myths and misunderstanding that can lead individuals to make ill-informed decisions jeopardizing their digital safety. The intent of this chapter is to peel back the layers of inaccuracy and shed a profound light on this crucial subject.

5.1. Understanding Privacy and Security on Social Media

An understanding of privacy and security is fundamental when it comes to the virtual realm of social media. The terms 'privacy' and 'security' might feel interchangeable, but they serve two distinct functions. Privacy pertains to the control over personal information and its protection against misuse, while security is all about the measures implemented to protect the data stored on digital platforms against unauthorized access, use, disclosure, disruption, modification, inspection, recording or destruction.

One common myth paints social media platforms as inherently insecure, often likening their use to walking through a digital minefield. However, the reality is that these platforms invest substantially in securing their user data. The advent of features like two-factor authentication and intricate encryption practices illustrates their commitment. These security measures certainly do not convert these platforms into digital fortresses but significantly enhance security levels.

5.2. Myth: "Social Media Companies Sell User Data"

A prominent misconception is that social media companies sell user data to advertisers, thereby compromising user privacy. The truth is more nuanced. Companies use the data to provide targeted advertising, customizing content based on the user's preferences shared on social media platforms. They do not sell raw data. Instead, they sell insights into the data: derived demographic information, behavior patterns, and targeted preference reports that allow advertisers to deliver more relevant adverts.

5.3. Myth: "Privacy Settings Guarantee Complete Privacy"

The belief that enabling privacy settings guarantees full privacy on social media is a common fallacy. These settings undoubtedly contribute to creating a private environment by controlling who sees your content and how your data is used. However, they do not offer ironclad protection. Even with the strictest privacy settings, elements such as profile pictures and cover photos on some platforms are generally public.

5.4. Myth: "Deleted Content is Gone Forever"

Users often assume that once a post is deleted, it's gone forever. This is not always the case. Deletion from the user's profile doesn't guarantee that the data isn't stored on social media servers or hasn't been screenshot and saved by another user. The impact of social media on data permanence is profound. It's crucial to be aware of this while sharing sensitive information online.

5.5. Importance of User Responsibility

While social media platforms must ensure sufficient security measures are in place, users also play a vital role in maintaining digital safety. A few tips include setting strong, unique passwords, enabling two-factor authentication, understanding privacy settings, being vigilant about sharing personal information, and regularly reviewing and updating security configurations.

5.6. Moving Beyond the Myths: A Call for Critical Awareness

In conclusion, though social media platforms do carry privacy and security concerns, the myths surrounding them often exaggerate and misrepresent these issues. Users need to be critically aware of these considerations, understanding that privacy and security in the digital realm is a shared responsibility. The first step is debunking the myths and facing the facts, a task this chapter aims to accomplish. Moving forward, a blend of increased awareness and informed action can lead to a safer, more secure social media experience.

Chapter 6. Fact-checking: The Role of Social Media in Spreading News

The proliferation of digital communication platforms like social media has taken information dissemination to a level of unprecedented immediacy and accessibility. However, as Plato, the enlightenment philosopher, once noted, with great power comes great responsibility. As we venture into this chapter, we'll meticulously examine the fact-checking mechanisms and the crucial role social media plays in spreading news, separating the engrained myths from the elusive truths.

6.1. The Phenomenon of Virality

The concept of virality bears an intrinsic relationship with the sphere of social media, and understanding this phenomenon is essential to lay the groundwork for our investigative journey. Drawing its roots from the medical terminology for the rapidly spreading nature of a virus, virality manifests itself in the digital space as the explosive spread of content—news articles, memes, videos, and more—across social media platforms. Theoretically, the speed at which the content disseminates is directly proportional to the amount of sharing it provokes within the user community.

However, the coin of virality flips onto its darker side when it becomes the vehicle for spreading false information or 'fake news.' With the increasing dependence on social media as our primary news source, this risk has markedly escalated. What makes this especially worrisome is the users' tendency to share content based on captivating headlines or emotional triggers, often without investigating the verity of the information.

6.2. Social Media Algorithms: An Unseen Hand

The decisive factor directing the virality and reach of information on social media is the generated algorithms. Through methods like machine learning and artificial intelligence, the algorithm curates a user's feed based on their preferences, interactions, and recently viewed content. This beneficence, however, can backfire as it creates an 'echo chamber,' reinforcing the user's existing biases and selectively amplifying content that aligns with the user's viewpoints.

Such 'filter bubbles' can dangerously skew the perception of reality, primarily when undifferentiated between facts and bias-confirming misinformation. This issue is worsened by the algorithm's ultimately impersonal nature; it perpetuates information viral propagation not based on its factual accuracy, but rather its potential for user engagement—from likes, shares or comments by users—leading to a cascade of misinformed narratives.

6.3. Fact-checking: A Profound Antidote to Misinformation

Identifying the growing threat of misinformation, some social media platforms have integrated fact-checking mechanisms. Fact-checking is a process where independent organizations or professionals scrutinize the credibility of information, particularly those circulating virally. The primary purpose is to verify the claims, cross-examine the sources, and subsequently flag or downplay misleading or false content.

Fact-checking combats the amplification of false narratives, protecting consumers of news on social media from being misguided by erroneous reports. However, this mechanism is not entirely foolproof and has been mired in controversies, including claims of bias, inaccuracy, or censorship.

6.4. The Role of User Responsibility

Ultimately, the role of social media in spreading news, either factual or false, underscores the substantial responsibility social media users should shoulder. Media literacy, including understanding how social media algorithms function and the implications of sharing unverified news, must be fosters. Treating headlines with skepticism, pausing before sharing, verifying from trusted sources, and considering the potential detrimental impacts of spreading false information, all form integral parts of responsible social media usage.

6.5. Shaping Forward: Toward an Informed and Discerning Social Media Landscape

The prevalence of fake news and the role of social media in its dissemination necessitate collective efforts from all stakeholders—platform providers, users, and fact-checkers. Social media companies should strive for transparent operations and enhance their fact-checking capabilities. Users need to develop digital literacy skills and adopt a more critical approach to consuming information. Fact-checkers must continue their vital role with utmost fairness and integrity.

In conclusion, the role of social media in spreading news is complex, multifaceted, and laden with responsibility. It is crucial to educate users and corporations about the truths and myths surrounding fact-checking and the influence of social media on information dissemination. By fostering a culture of fact-checking and digital literacy, we can mitigate the spread of misinformation and strengthen our collective apprehension of reality in the digital age. In this way, we can hope for a refined, discerning social media landscape.

Chapter 7. Influencers and Their Impact: Behind the Myths

In the ever-expanding realm of social media, influencers have come to occupy significant positions of influence and power, dictating trends, swaying consumer behaviors, and driving public opinion. But, the veil of myths shrouding the reality of this profession and its impacts necessitates a rigorous inspection in an attempt to separate the chaff of falsities from the wheat of truth. This chapter seeks to delve into the complex web of myths surrounding social media influencers and their impact and to unravel the facts that lie beneath.

7.1. The Birth and Rise of the Influencer Phenomenon

Social media influencers—those individuals who, armed with a strong online presence, wield their persuasive power to shape consumer behavior and preferences—rose to prominence with the boom that social media experienced in the late 2000s. Origination as bloggers, vloggers, and early adopters of platforms like Instagram and Snapchat, these individuals capitalized on their follower counts and personal branding strategies to begin a new era of digital influence. But as the space transformed, so did the conceptions and misconceptions about it. It's crucial to understand this historical context to fully comprehend the present scenarios and debunk the myths circulating about influencers and their impact.

7.2. Untangling the Web of Myths about Influencers

One common misconception is that influencers lead a luxurious, effortless life, merely posting pictures or videos on social media. However, the reality is significantly more complex. The art of influencing necessitates a colossal amount of labor: it involves careful content creation and curation, strategic planning, constant engagement with their audiences, and continual learning of updated platform algorithms.

Another rampant myth is the supposedly low impacting nature of influencers. Contrary to this belief, numerous studies and economic figures indicate the considerable magnitude of the influencer marketing industry. According to the Influencer Marketing Hub, the market size is estimated to reach $13.8 billion in 2021, highlighting the profound role influencers play in shaping purchasing decisions.

7.3. The Power and Pitfalls of Influencer Marketing

Influencer marketing, when strategically implemented, can yield substantial gains. They offer a human connection that's often lost in traditional advertising, their content can reach niche markets, and they often possess an authenticity that resonates with audiences.

However, alongside these benefits are challenges. The potential for inauthentic partnerships, the risk of misinformation, and controversy surrounding transparency, notably concerning paid partnerships, contribute to a clouded perception of the impact of influencer marketing. Hence the assertion that all influencer marketing is successful is a myth.

7.4. The Ethical Implications of Influencing

Another myth that pervades the influencer sphere is the dismissal of the ethical implications of their work. Influencers, given their sway over large audiences, inherently bear a significant amount of responsibility in ensuring accurate and honest communication and promoting healthy behaviors and standards.

7.5. Influencers and Mental Health

There's a circulating misconception that influencers are immune to the mental health strains often associated with intense social media use. However, influencers, too, can experience the negative psychological effects of social media, such as online harassment, anxiety, depression, and burnout. The notion of them being an unaffected class is a myth that needs debunking.

The task of busting the myths about social media influencers requires a comprehensive understanding of the context and conscientious analysis of the facts. While these online personalities are undeniably potent and impactful, dissecting the realities from the myths ensures a more balanced perspective on the influencers and their significant role in the social media landscape.

Having delved into the meat of the subject, this subchapter's exploration hopefully fosters a more informed, realistic understanding of the intricacies woven into the tapestry of social media influencers, their work, and impact on society. They are not merely individuals with large followings but powerful elements in the vast, ever-changing macrocosm of social media.

Chapter 8. The Truth About Social Media and Business Marketing

The universe of social media has become an integral fixture in today's marketing strategies for businesses. A tool of unprecedented reach and power, social media platforms allow companies to engage directly with their target demographic, gather valuable consumer data, and market their products and services with a level of specificity and personalization previously undreamt of. However, as with any powerful tool, social media's role in business marketing is shrouded in misconceptions and myths. This section aims to give an exhaustive rundown of these myths, debunking them one by one and elucidating the true impact and role of social media in contemporary business marketing.

8.1. Myth: Social Media is Not for B2B Businesses

It is often believed that social media marketing only works for business-to-consumer (B2C) organizations, while business-to-business (B2B) companies do not stand to gain anything from their presence on these platforms. This could not be farther from the truth. Although traditional promotional methods continue to be primary drivers in B2B relation-building, social media platforms—particularly professional networking sites like LinkedIn—can provide significant benefits in terms of creating brand awareness and thought leadership, strengthening customer relationships, and generating leads.

8.2. Myth: Businesses Must be Present on Every Social Media Platform

Many businesses labor under the misconception that they need to have a presence on every social media platform to maximize their reach. However, an effective social media strategy does not necessarily involve being everywhere at once. Rather, businesses should focus on identifying those platforms where their targeted demographic are most likely to spend their time and tailor their strategies accordingly. It's about quality engagement, not quantity.

8.3. Myth: More Followers Equates to More Business Success

Another prevalent myth is that the success of social media marketing is defined purely by the number of followers a business has. While having a large follower count can certainly boost visibility, it does not necessarily equate to increased conversion rates or sales. The focus should be on fostering a solid community of engaged followers interested in your products and services, as this will invariably encourage loyalty and word-of-mouth recommendations.

8.4. Myth: Social Media Leads to Immediate Sales

Many businesses enter the social media space with a misunderstanding that sharing a few posts will lead to instant conversions and sales, which is far from reality. Building a successful social media strategy is a long-term commitment. It requires time, consistency, and effort in engaging with your audience, building trust, showing your brand personality and value before translating into tangible results.

8.5. Myth: Social Media Can't Drive Leads and Sales

Contrarily to the aforementioned myth, there is also a belief that social media can't drive leads and sales at all. While the impact of social media may not be as direct as other forms of marketing, when used effectively it can create a loyal community around your brand, foster trust, and gently push followers along the sales funnel by showcasing products, services, and company values.

Social media's role in business marketing is complex and multifaceted. It wields immense power to shape consumer perception and sentiment towards brands, and thus must be treated with a stratagem that goes beyond surface-level myths. Understanding the true nature of social media in business marketing can equip organizations with the knowledge to employ their resources effectively and harness the real potential of this digital arena. As we have highlighted, it's not about being everywhere, gaining hollow followers, anticipating immediate sales, or dismissing it as a non-lead generating tool. It's about thoughtful engagement, meticulous strategy and understanding the intricate dynamics of digital consumer behavior.

Chapter 9. Myth vs. Reality: The Effect of Social Media on Relationships

Social media, by its very nature, thrives on relationships. It seeks to connect us, to foster communication, to bridge the gap between distance and time. Yet, as with any powerful tool, it is susceptible to abuse, misuse, and misunderstanding. Therefore, in order to arrive at a well-rounded comprehension of the effects of social media on relationships, we need to sift fact from fiction, to separate prevalent myths from harsh realities.

9.1. Social Media and Interpersonal Relationships: A New Public Sphere

The dawn of social media platforms ushered in an era of digital communities, a public sphere redefined. Where, traditionally, public communication took place in physical forums – town squares, cafés, university campuses – the 21st century has seen the animation of a grand digital colloquium. This new sphere, however, comes with its own dynamics and impacts on social relationships.

The myth posits that social media relationships are superficial, lacking depth and genuine connection. However, the reality reveals a more nuanced picture. Yes, social media can give rise to ephemeral relationships, with users accruing 'friends' or 'followers' with the click of a button. Yet, this broad networking capacity also fosters opportunities for renewed connections, for solidarity in the face of shared experiences, for support across physical boundaries. It is therefore necessary to understand the multifaceted nature of digital social interactions in order to navigate this new public sphere effectively.

9.2. Social Media and the Dialectics of Visibility and Privacy

One of the significant aspects of digital interactions in social media is the dialectics of visibility and privacy. On one hand, social media platforms offer spaces for self-presentation, for 'being seen'. On the other hand, the visibility often comes at the price of privacy since personal information is widely accessible to the digital community.

A prevalent myth in this regard is that if one wants to guard their privacy, it's best to abstain from any social media platform. However, this binary view neglects the fact that social media also offers options for privacy settings that allow users to control the visibility of their content. Realising the existence of this greater measure of control, users are free to balance their needs for social connectivity with their desires for personal privacy.

9.3. The Commodification of Relationships

In the digital age, where data is the new oil, our activities on social media platforms feed into massive databases. These data are then packaged and sold to advertisers and businesses interested in targeted marketing.

There is a myth that this commodification of relationships doesn't affect us significantly in our personal lives. Yet, the reality is that commodification not only leads to intrusive advertising, but it also algorithmically shapes the content that we see on our social media feeds. Consequently, we're exposed more to certain kinds of posts, people, and opinions, subtly influencing our perceptions and behaviours within our social relationships.

9.4. Social Media and Emotional Health

The link between our emotional health and social media use is a complex web of interactions. The myth that social media inherently leads to feelings of inadequacy, jealousy, or anxiety represents only surface-level understanding.

In reality, while some people may experience such negative emotions due to disproportionate consumption of idealised realities, others find solace, support, and validation on these platforms. The impact of social media on our emotional health, thus, isn't binary—it's contingent on numerous individual and contextual factors such as duration of use, type of content consumed, individual predispositions, and existing support systems.

9.5. The Double-Edged Sword of Connectivity

Social media, with its ubiquitous presence, has shrunk the world into a virtual village, challenging long held beliefs about distance and relationships. Connectivity has become an oxymoron; the myth proposes the idea that increased digital connectivity necessarily means decreased 'real-world' connectivity.

However, the reality isn't as clear-cut. While it's undeniable that excessive screen-time can encroach upon in-person interaction, social media also aids in signalling social reinforcement, provides tools for strengthening bonds across geographies, and acts as a lifeline in these unprecedented times of global crises.

In summary, the ultimate impact of social media on our relationships is not predetermined or universally applicable—it depends greatly on mindful, informed use. By distinguishing these prevalent myths from realities, we're better equipped to wield the power of social media to our advantage, to truly connect in the digital age, to harness its capabilities without falling prey to its pitfalls.

In the succeeding chapters, we'll further delve into strategies for responsible and informed social media use, offering tips to navigate this vast digital landscape with clarity and confidence.

Chapter 10. Busting Myths About Social Media and Cyberbullying

Cyberbullying, an unfortunate but all too common phenomenon, has morphed and proliferated with the rise of social media, taking on new dimensions that require careful analysis and understanding. Current conversations are often rife with misconceptions about the nature, extent, and ways to tackle this metaphorical virus of the virtual world. This chapter seeks to burst the bubble of these myths, helping to arm us with knowledge that can lead to effective solutions.

10.1. Understanding Cyberbullying

To properly debunk myths, we first need a solid understanding of what cyberbullying entails. In its simplest form, cyberbullying is the use of digital technologies, particularly social media, to harass, threaten, embarrass or target another person. This form of bullying can occur through SMS, Text, apps, or online in social media, forums, or gaming where people can view, participate in, or share the content.

Unlike traditional bullying, cyberbullying can occur 24 hours a day and seven days a week, and the bully can remain anonymous if they choose, leading to potentially severe psychological effects on the victim.

10.2. Debunking the Prevalent Myths about Cyberbullying

10.2.1. Myth 1: "Just turn off the computer or smartphone."

Many people believe that the solution to cyberbullying is as simple as disconnecting from the offending platform. However, this view neglects a crucial aspect of the modern digital age - the internet is now deeply fused with our personal, academic, and professional lives. Literally disconnecting is, for many people, practically impossible. Furthermore, this approach simply forces victims to limit their activities and doesn't address the root problem, that is, the bully's behaviour.

10.2.2. Myth 2: "Cyberbullying is less damaging than physical bullying."

Although cyberbullying may lack a physical component, suggesting that it is less damaging is a dangerous misconception. The psychological and emotional impact of cyberbullying can last for a long time, leading to anxieties, depression, and tragically, even self-harming behaviours in some cases. It's often more widespread, intrusive, and relentless compared to traditional forms of bullying.

10.2.3. Myth 3: "Only teenagers are victims of cyberbullying."

While it's true that many instances of cyberbullying occur among younger age groups due to their frequent use of social media, it is a mistake to believe that adults are immune. Today, businesses, celebrities, politicians, and everyday citizens face a variety of cyberbullying forms including trolling, doxing, cancel culture, and online harassment.

10.3. Possible Solutions and Strategies

Now that we've effectively dispelled some of the prevalent myths about cyberbullying, it's essential to move toward solutions. Both proactive and reactive approaches are necessary to curb this social epidemic effectively.

10.3.1. Digital Literacy and Cyber Ethics

Promoting digital literacy and cyberspace ethics is a proactive way to tackle the issue. Both young people and adults need to understand the real consequences of their online actions and the potential harm they can inflict on others.

10.3.2. Internet Regulation and Social Media Policies

Governments worldwide and social media platforms need to enforce stringent laws and regulations to punish cyberbullies. The platforms themselves should work towards advanced moderation and reporting options, making their platforms safer and more inclusive for all users.

10.3.3. Encouragement of Reporting

Victims and witnesses of cyberbullying need to know that their voices matter. They should be encouraged to report such behaviour to relevant authorities, whether school administrators, workplace teams, or platform moderators.

In conclusion, the task of busting myths about cyberbullying involves us all in a collective effort to create a safer, kinder virtual world. By equipping ourselves with the facts, challenging our perceptions, and working towards proactive and responsive solutions, we can bring about real change in the social media landscape.

Chapter 11. Moving Forward: Strategies for Responsible and Informed Social Media Use

As we plunge towards the closing sections of this enlightening report, our exploration now shifts to more practical and user-oriented aspects of our social media engagement; specifically, strategies for responsible and informed social media use. During our journey so far, we've debunked several social media myths related to algorithms, privacy, mental health, news dissemination, influencers, and even commerces' intersection with these platforms. This effort has cleared a path for more enlightened and enlightened social media interaction. However, it also unveils a pressing question: How should we practically apply this newfound knowledge for more responsible and informed social media use?

11.1. The Principles of Responsible Social Media Use

Principles form an essential pillar of any navigation system, and it's no different when dealing with a complex landscape like social media. They serve as a guiding compass to lead us safely and considerately through the virtual maze.

The first principle of responsible use is mindful and deliberate engagement. This means not simply absorbing and sharing content at face value, but seeking to understand the context and implications of any material we interact with. Discerning real news from fake, evaluating the credibility of sources, and considering the potential repercussions of our digital engagements helps reduce the spread of false or harmful information.

The second is respect for privacy. Understanding your social media platform's settings and controls can help manage the audience for your posts, providing a level of control over what is shared and with whom. It's also worth remembering that respecting privacy extends to other users; sharing or commenting on other people's posts should be done responsibly.

Finally, there is the principle of constructive involvement. Social media platforms are, at heart, meant to facilitate communication and connections. Using these platforms to build rather than break, to support rather than vilify, and to share rather than hoard, fosters a healthier digital environment.

11.2. The Importance of Digital Well-being

As we become increasingly enmeshed in the digital age, the concept of digital well-being has emerged as another essential element to consider. Digital well-being refers to the impact of technology and digital services on people's mental, physical and emotional health. It includes understanding and managing the time spent on digital platforms, mitigating the risks of digital dependency, and fostering a healthier relationship with technology.

On social media, this might look like setting clearly defined boundaries for usage time, regularly detoxing or taking breaks from digital platforms, and being mindful of the quality of the content consumed. It's about creating balance in our lives, where digital interactions complement rather than dominate our real-world experiences.

11.3. Fact-checking and Critical Thinking

Critical thinking is another indispensable skill when navigating the modern digital terrain. It involves scrutinizing the information we encounter rather than passively receiving it. Key questions to ponder might include: Is the source reputable? Is the information biased or impartial? Who benefits from the shared information or narrative?

Fact-checking is a crucial aspect of this process. It can be achieved by cross-referencing the information with reputable sources, verifying it through dedicated fact-checking organizations, and questioning the origins of viral posts.

11.4. Developing a Personal Social Media Strategy

A personal social media strategy can assist greatly in achieving responsible and informed use of these platforms. Such a strategy may involve a defined set of goals pertaining to what you want to achieve from your social media use, the adoption of specific practices to promote digital well-being, strategies to respect privacy, and approaches to engage mindfully and constructively on the platforms.

The elements of the strategy should align with your personal needs, lifestyle, and online interactions. It's a personalized navigation blueprint for your digital life that can significantly enhance the quality of your online engagements.

To sum up, responsible and informed social media use is a multifaceted endeavor. It's about combining broad principles, an awareness of digital well-being, critical thinking faculties, and a crafted personal social media strategy. As we continue our dance with the digital age, understanding these aspects and integrating them effectively into our social media interactions will empower us to relish the rhythm and avoid pitfalls on this digital dance floor. Ultimately, the goal is to cultivate an online environment that respects human dignity, encourages truthful dialogue, and contributes to a healthier digital society.

www.ingramcontent.com/pod-product-compliance
Lightning Source LLC
LaVergne TN
LVHW051633050326
832903LV00033B/4739